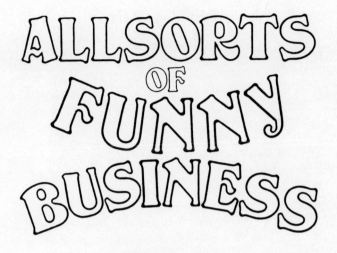

ALLSORTS OF FUNNY BUSINESS

compiled by
Annabel Allott
in aid of
The British Heart Foundation

edited by Rupert Morris

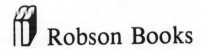 Robson Books

DEDICATION

For Louise

First published in Great Britain in 1989 by Robson Books Ltd,
Bolsover House, 5–6 Clipstone Street, London W1P 7EB

Copyright © 1989 Annabel Allott

British Library Cataloguing in Publication Data
All sorts of funny business.
    1. Humorous prose in English – 1945 Anthologies
    I. Allott, Annabel
    828'.91407'08

    ISBN 0 86051 605 9

Printed in Great Britain by T.J. Press (Padstow) Ltd, Padstow, Cornwall.

CONTENTS

ACKNOWLEDGEMENTS

I would like to thank Jonathan Shack, Dick Askwith, Stephen Allott, Len Heath, Hugh Bredin, Brian Palmer, Corynne Bredin, Anthea Davies and Lucy Mobbs for their help and support. Special thanks should go to Caren Bramley, Tina Black and Rebecca Ashton who helped with the typing. All the cartoonists who gave their time and skills so willingly and to Rupert Morris who helped with the editing.

Finally, thanks to New Solutions and The Food Business who let me use 'office' time so generously.

Chapter 1

The Entertainment and Media Business

TERRY WOGAN
Presenter
BBC

Elton John was my guest on Monday 18 February 1985. It was the first of the new thrice weekly *Wogans* broadcast live from the BBC Television Theatre at Shepherd's Bush.

The credits rolled, and I left my chair to walk over and greet Elton, who was standing by the piano. As I reached forward to shake hands, I tripped, staggered for a moment, groped vainly in his direction, and fell in an ungainly heap on the floor. Ever the gentleman, Elton moved downstage to help me to my feet. It wasn't quite the introduction we had in mind.

'Typical of Wogan! He'll go to any lengths to upstage a guest.'

LENNY HENRY
Comedian

The year is 1977. I am booked into a summer season at Felixstowe for 10 weeks with a man renowned for his funkiness, grooviness and complete and utter cruciality. I refer, of course, to John Hanson, he of 'Desert Songs' fame – yes, the Red Shadow.

It is the fifth week. I know everybody in the cast: Peter Butterworth, from the *Carry On* films, a Mexican trio who taught me rude words in Spanish, John Hanson, of course, and finally Ann-Marie and Louise, an animal magic act who can conjure a dog from a washing machine, a cat from a tin of baked beans, pigeons from the back of the theatre etc.

They have a very big parrot called Miggs and sometimes you can hear him before the show laughing a loud and piercing laugh like Harry Secombe in the *Goon Show*.

I am waiting by the side of the stage, in plenty of time for my big number with John and Peter. It is that old showbiz chestnut 'Friendship' – you know the one: 'Whenever friendships have been forgot, ours will still be hot'.

As I wait, John is regaling the audience of grey-haired, adoring old ladies with tales of his appearances on shows with Morecambe and Wise and Des O'Connor. All of a sudden, Miggs, obviously tickled by the cumulative weight of five weeks of these anecdotes, lets out this amazingly human sounding laugh that goes on for about two minutes.

I beg the parrot to stop, but it keeps going. Eventually, they tie a rubber band around its beak. The Red Shadow is not amused, and because I am waiting at the side of the stage, thinks I am responsible. He storms off-stage well

before the end of 'Friendship, Friendship' and I get a note in my dressing room afterwards demanding an apology. When John finds out the truth it is I who get the apology.

But the experience has put me off parrots for life. I might make an exception for one sautéd in an onion and tomato sauce with perhaps a hint of chilli!

ALAN H PROTHEROE MBE
Assistant Director General
BBC

The BBC loves to use acronyms to identify its managers. The Director General, for example, is always referred to as 'DG'; the Managing Director of External Broadcasting as 'MDXB', and the Head of Current Affairs Magazine Programmes rejoices in the title 'H-CAMP'.

When I was Assistant Director General of the BBC, I had to preview a *Panorama* programme at the Lime Grove studios early one Sunday morning.

My chauffeur-driven car swept up to the barrier, and the driver told the security man, 'ADG for *Panorama*'.

The barrier swung up; the car swept in.

I was greeted at the *Panorama* office not merely by smiling faces but by loud guffaws. The security man had telephoned the office to say: 'The man from the KGB is on his way up . . .'

JULIAN LLOYD WEBBER

Musician

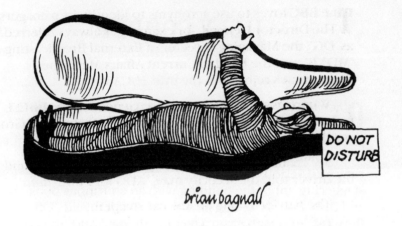

brian bagnall

Sponsorship of 'celebrity concerts' has become quite a sport in business circles and I was performing at a splendid provincial theatre where the local backers insisted that a 'slap-up' feast be held after the performance at a local restaurant known for its *haute cuisine*.

But I had another idea.

Close to the concert hall there was a magnificent pub serving ale from the cask and a juicy, chewy, succulent Welsh Rarebit over the bar. I had been let in on their secret a year or so previously, and nothing was going to prevent a long-overdue return. So the excuses were made – I was tired and had to be fresh for tomorrow's rehearsal – and I set off happily to the pub.

Several pints and a couple of Welsh Rarebits later my reveries were disturbed by a tap on the shoulder. The sponsors had finished their meal and arrived for a little 'nightcap'.

JILLY COOPER
Author/Journalist

Office life has its compensations. Like the occasion when Billy Collins, the splendid head of William Collins the publishers, sacked a friend of mine called Bernard. For the next month as he was working out his notice, Bernard removed various pieces of office property. One day he was staggering out of the building with an enormous bookcase, and Billy Collins, seeing he was overloaded, said: 'Oh Bernard, let me give you a hand with that.' And proceeded to help him carry the bookcase out to his van. I am pleased to say that Bernard has done very well since.

JEREMY IRONS
Actor

My wife and I went to a matinée of a West End musical. After the performance we went backstage to see some of the cast. On our way out of the theatre, we got into conversation with someone about the show. We said we felt that although the actors had performed heroically, the choreography was so naïve, banal, old-fashioned and clichéd as to confound all their efforts.

We were, of course, careful, since our acquaintance had presumably been visiting a cast member, not to single out any performer's name. As my wife and I said our goodbyes and walked off down Shaftesbury Avenue I asked her the lady's name. 'I don't know. Wasn't she a friend of yours?' she said.

At that moment, in a blinding flash, it came to me who she was – she was the choreographer!

ANTHONY B M GOOD
Chairman
Good Relations Group PLC

We had been briefing the management of a major hotel on the importance of 'crisis planning and management' and suggested that a manual and briefing procedure should be established for disasters of all kinds.

A few days after our conversation, a carload of terrorists drove past and machine-gunned the windows of the ground floor restaurant, causing no little alarm (though fortunately no serious injuries) to the diners inside.

Next morning the General Manager called us: 'It wasn't really necessary,' he said, 'to go to such lengths to get your point across.'

MICHAEL GAMBON
Actor

I was having dinner with a TV director some years ago and about to start rehearsing a TV play with him the following morning.

We were chatting away and I told him that I'd just seen the most awful film.

I said the actors were so wooden that they seemed to be appearing by kind arrangement with the Forestry

Commission and the Director ought to be shot!

He asked me what it was called; I told him and gave him even more details.

Months later I found out that he had directed it.

He never said a word. Whenever I think of this, it makes me shiver.

THE RIGHT HON LORD HAVERS
Former Attorney-General

In my first murder case I was junior counsel to Peter Rawlinson (now Lord Rawlinson), representing a man called Whiteway. It was a sensational trial in its day and attracted a lot of press attention. Despite our efforts the defendant was convicted. He was sentenced immediately and so, within half an hour of the jury's verdict, I was leaving the Old Bailey. As I crossed the road I was astonished to see that the headline on the newspapers being sold from a small stand there was 'Whiteway Convicted'. I asked the paper seller, 'How on earth did the papers know about the verdict so quickly?' 'It was easy, sir,' he replied, and pointed to a bundle of newspapers on the pavement behind the stand, with the headline 'Whiteway Acquitted',

JANE ASHER
Actress

Actors must never allow an audience to catch them laughing – or 'corpsing' as we call it – particularly if they are unaware of the cause. But there are times when events on stage become so excruciatingly funny that the more you try to pull yourself together and be professional, the more you shake with helpless laughter.

A few years ago I was touring in a rather strange play called *Ophelia* by C P Taylor. It used the *Hamlet* characters to explore the enclosed and mysterious world of the schizophrenic – in this case Ophelia.

On reflection I think it was a pretty pretentious play, but when you are working on something you have to suspend disbelief in order to do justice to the author.

One theatre where we were booked to play was very small and our set would only just fit. The space was so tight that there was no room behind the set, or on either side where the wings would normally be.

When a member of the cast had to exit from one side of the stage and re-enter later from the other, as if from a different room of the castle, he would have to leave the building by the side door, race round the back along a cobbled alleyway, and then come back into the theatre on the other side and so re-enter the action.

As the schizophrenic Ophelia I spent the entire play on-stage and so was spared this circuitous route.

On our second night I said farewell to a departing Hamlet and then, after delivering a particularly sad, long and moving monologue, turned to welcome his return from another part of the castle.

An extraordinary, bedraggled, dripping figure

confronted me and with a sudden panic I realized it must be raining heavily.

Various separate ad libs raced through my brain but were quickly rejected: 'Hast thou taken a shower my Lord?' or 'The roof of the ante-room, it leaketh?' The sight of a soggy Hamlet trying in all seriousness to speak his intense and heartfelt lines, coupled with the murmurings from the audience puzzled as to the author's intention in suddenly presenting Hamlet soaking wet with no explanation, proved too much for me, and I had to turn upstage and hope that my shaking shoulders looked as if I was racked with sobs.

After several more characters had entered in a similar condition and the cast were all twitching with badly-suppressed mirth, the audience began to suspect that something was even more rotten than usual in the state of Denmark and that it had not been C P Taylor's intention to present this drenched court at Elsinore.

From then on they were on our side, and although the play may have lost some of its more serious observations on schizophrenia, it acquired a speed, loudness and intensity of concentration that it had never had before.

DAVID LANGTON

Actor

In the play *The Pleasure of His Company* at the
Haymarket Theatre, I was playing Jim Dougherty, the
second husband of Coral Browne. Nigel Patrick was
playing her first husband who arrives at our home, in San
Francisco, to give away his daughter in marriage. Coral
Browne, who was known as the best dressed actress on the
London stage, wore a stunning black dress by Balmain. The
accessories were perfect; she looked sensational. One
night she made her entrance on stage to the usual

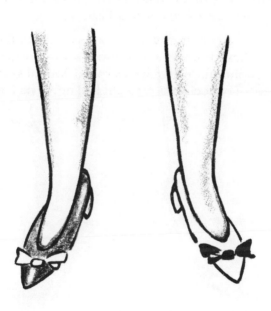

approving murmurs from the audience, but this time a few giggles, too. She was wearing one black shoe and one brown shoe! Nigel Patrick spotted the mistake and deliberately stared and smirked at her feet for far too long. Eventually she glanced down at her feet and all but fainted, then with great dignity walked slowly upstage and stood behind the sofa for the rest of the long scene. She refused to budge. When she came off-stage her language almost cracked the walls of the Haymarket.

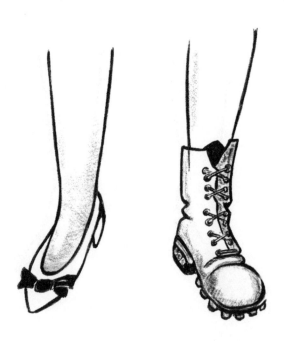

DEREK JACOBI
Actor

The part that made me, a good few years ago, was that of the stammering Emperor Claudius in the BBC series, *I Claudius*. Much more recently, I appeared in a play called *Breaking the Code* about the computer expert Alan Turing who also had an impediment in his speech.

The following conversation was overheard in the play's interval:

1st American: 'This play sure is something.'
2nd American: 'Yeah, sure, and this actor Derek Jacobi sure is something too.'
1st American: 'You're right, but I don't suppose he gets much work with that bad stutter!'

'The trouble is that whenever a report comes out linking smoking with heart disease, he smokes more to calm his nerves ...'

Chapter 2

The
Retail
Business

LORD SIEFF OF BRIMPTON
Chairman
Marks and Spencer PLC

My father got to know people at the Vatican in the sixties, and became friendly with a leading Cardinal.

Two or three years later the telephone rang when I happened to be in father's office. It was the Cardinal on the telephone who said: 'Israel, I rang you up in case you were worried.'

Father said: 'Worried about what?' The Cardinal said: 'I thought you might be worried because we are regrading the Saints.'

Father asked: 'Regrading the Saints, what on earth do you mean?' To which the Cardinal replied: 'We are downgrading a number of Saints – we are not upgrading any. For example, St Christopher becomes a lower ranking Saint, but I phoned to assure you we are not touching St Michael.'

SIR TERENCE CONRAN
Chairman and CEO
Storehouse Group

True Story:
Woman comes up to sales desk of Habitat in Manchester with carrier bag full of broken glass. Customer: 'Your spaghetti jars don't work.'

Salesgirl: 'Why?'

Customer: 'I put it on top of the stove with the spaghetti covered with water, but when I turned on the gas, the glass shattered.'

Salesgirl: 'Why on earth did you do that?'

Customer: 'It was too tall to go in the oven!'

JEFFREY ARCHER
Author

When I was a young man I borrowed £50,000 from the bank to purchase a long lease on a building in Grafton Street for the purpose of opening an art gallery. I selected all the artists I admired, and worked night and day to make the gallery a success, but quickly found I had neither the expertise nor the background to challenge the professional gallery owners all around me.

By the end of my first year as an art dealer, I had lost a further £50,000 and my bank manager quite rightly suggested that I should stop dealing, as his bank was not in the business of pouring money into an obviously useless venture. Dejected by the thought of losing £100,000, but realizing that there was no way out, I gave the three members of staff a month's notice with full pay, closed the doors and asked my accountant to work out the full losses after we had returned the canvases to the artists concerned and disposed of the lease.

All this was put in hand a few days before I went on summer holiday with my family.

When I returned a month later I found a cheque for £107 on my desk. My solicitor assured me that this was the profit after all the bills had been dealt with on my art gallery venture. Obviously thinking there had been some horrendous mistake, I began to check over the figures carefully – only to discover that the gallery lease had been sold to an antique dealer for £120,000.

This was how I learned that really shrewd people do not open art galleries when they can be property speculators.

MILES KINGTON
Author

When I was a lad, I spotted an advertisement in a paper which read as follows:

'Peer or gentleman with title needed to work with modern go-ahead concern'.

Well, I had always heard that putting Lord so-and-so on your letter-heading could add half a million pounds to your turnover, so I wrote back a letter as follows:

Dear Sir,

Although not a Lord in my own right, I was given the unusual christian name of 'Lord' by my father who foresaw that this would be of great help to me in commercial life, as very few people would be able to tell the difference between me and a real Lord. I have just left school and am ready to begin, if you are ready to put me on your letter-heading.

Yours,
Lord Kington

To my surprise, I received a letter from the go-ahead concern (it turned out to be a large antique shop in Brighton) which was full of enthusiasm for my ideas. They suggested meeting for lunch in London with a view to putting me on their board of directors, or whatever antique shops have. My nerve failed me, and I never replied or went to have lunch with them. But when my father read the exchange letters, he said to me: 'Just as well. You would have made a rotten businessman. But judging from your letter, you've got a chance as a humorous writer. Why not give that a go?'

I did, and now I am almost rich enough to be able to buy an antique in Brighton!

JAMES GULLIVER
Chairman
Argyll Group

We were opening the first out-of-town giant food store in Britain in 1970. The opening was at 10.00 a.m. and at 9.55 a.m. the car park was jammed full, queues outside the store were enormous, a dixieland jazz band was playing at the entrance and the red ribbon was about to be cut by a TV celebrity. Inside, the store was merchandised and stocked to perfection. At 9.59 a.m., as the doors were due to open, we were plunged into darkness. In my anguish I reached out to touch a brand new cash register and exclaimed: 'God help us!' – and the lights went on!

TIM DALE
Recruitment and Training Controller
Harrods

It was a busy morning on the cheese counter, and a relative newcomer had been left in the buyer's office to deal with the telephone enquiries.

Suddenly a voice at the other end caused the colour to drain from the young lady's face. 'Just hold the line one minute please and I'll fetch the buyer,' she said nervously. She hurried into the department to find the buyer. 'It's them!' she whispered, 'It's Buckingham Palace and they want 18 lbs of cheddar.'

The buyer excused himself from the queue of customers and returned briskly to his office to take the call. A few minutes later he reappeared and took the young newcomer aside.

'You did the right thing,' he reassured her, 'but just so as you know for future occasions, The Prince of Wales is a pub on the other side of Brompton Road.'

TIM SAINSBURY MP

House of Commons

Because I was elected to the House at a by-election in November 1973, and there were two general elections in 1974, Hove experienced three full election campaigns in less than a year.

One housewife, on hearing her doorbell rung yet again

by a campaigner for the third election 'on behalf of Tim Sainsbury, your Conservative candidate', replied: 'Not this week, thank you.'

MICHAEL TRIPP
Director
Premier Brands Foodservice

One of our salesmen was on holiday and a relief salesman was sent to cover his calls.

In one outlet he was advised by a member of the staff that the manager was in an office at the back of the kitchens.

At the rear of the buildings he saw the head of a person (who, he assumed, was the manager) through the window, but he couldn't find a door to get in.

After waiting for several minutes, he tapped on the window. 'What do you want?' was shouted back. The salesman explained his business, but the manager said he was busy and didn't want anything.

The relief salesman persisted until the manager told him to go away in no uncertain terms.

The next time the regular salesman came round, the manager asked him who had taken his place the week before. 'I don't know,' was the reply. 'Why do you ask?'

'Well, he had certainly been trained to be persistent,' said the manager. 'There I was sitting on the lavatory and there was a tap on the window ...'

ALAN COTTON
Chairman and Managing Director
Bear Brand Hosiery

To celebrate 'London Stores Week' we decided to feature a live bear in the hosiery department of a leading department store. We thought we might upstage Pretty Polly, who were providing a live parrot.

Unfortunately, the bear died the day before he was due in-store. The replacement bear was completely uncontrollable and the model girl, who was booked to handle this supposedly 'friendly animal', was so frightened that she refused to take part.

While a special handler was summoned, the rampaging bear was quickly emptying the hosiery department. After our bear had made several attempts at eating the parrot, we decided to dispense with his services.

We didn't sell much hosiery that day, but for the life of me I cannot understand why we lost the account!

SIMON ARCHER
Corporate Communications Officer
Kodak

A customer wrote to us complaining that he had found insects on the glass screen of his single lens reflex camera.

He was right: the offending creatures, we discovered, were cheese-mites. They are harmless beasts, but viewed under magnification, through a pentaprism, they appear quite monstrous.

'Personally,' wrote the customer, 'I don't mind the little fellows, but I lent the camera to my mother-in-law, and they nearly frightened her to death.'

MICHAEL HOLROYD
Author

Some years ago I arrived at a Literature Festival in failing light and pouring rain. I was met by my Quixote of a publisher and together we paddled towards a barrow that had been loaded with a few sodden copies of books and took up our positions, like out-of-work gardeners, at each end. From the warm, dry interior of a tent sounds of a rival attraction (CoCo the Clown) floated out to us. We, shivering, held our ground. At last, in a desperate bid for attention and in defiance of several by-laws, my publisher commandeered a megaphone through which he bellowed with an air of panic that the 'world famous biographer' was even now signing copies of his books. 'Roll up!' he despaired. 'Roll up!'

The rain pelted down and no one rolled up. Then, through the gloom, a heavily mackintoshed figure emerged with a bundle. He splashed towards me. I drew my pen. He unpacked from the bundle a book of mine which, he volunteered, was not worth the paper it was written on (a statement which, in the downpour, became increasingly objectionable). Haughtily, I refused to buy it back. He insisted – and a fierce tug-of-war-in-reverse developed between us during which, in a moment of pyrrhic triumph, I inserted my signature. High above these two strangers struggling in the dark, my publisher kept up his insistent chanting. At length my anonymous reader rolled off, leaving my battered book behind him; and when the publisher returned I had to admit that I had scored minus one.

Chapter 3

The
Health
Business

JOHN COLE
Political Editor
BBC

A couple of months after I returned from work following a coronary artery by-pass operation, I was at the Conservative Party Conference in Brighton when the IRA bombing took place. I tumbled out of bed (in the hotel next door), and was soon on my way to the police station to interview Mrs Thatcher, who had been taken there. I then worked through the rest of the day till the nine o'clock news, was driven back to London, and got to bed, quite tired, at midnight.

The following week I had to phone the Westminster hospital to make an outpatient follow-up appointment. The Sister in my former ward – fully as old as my second son, but recently a figure of immense authority in my life – said: 'Hello, John. I saw you on the nine o'clock news that night. That's not the kind of working day we recommend.' I told the cardiologist of this conversation the following week. He laughed at his Sister's zeal, but said: 'I guess many of our patients behave as foolishly as you, but to do it in front of television cameras attracts our attention.'

STEPHEN WELLS
Managing Director
Connexions Group

Yet another market research survey on high fibre health foods.

It seemed as if people in the South liked such foods.

Northerners felt rather differently.

Asked to explain why high fibre food might be popular in the South but not the North, one woman replied: 'It's simple, this is just the sort of idea that would appeal to those "sedimentary" people down South.'

TOM JAGO
New Product Consultant
The Distillers Group

Prior to launching a new drink, IDV did some research to see if the taste appealed.

First woman: 'Yuck!'
Second woman: 'It's like cod liver oil!'
Third woman: 'Is it good for indigestion because it certainly isn't good for me!'

The results were suppressed, and shortly afterwards Baileys Irish Cream was launched.

SEDIMENTARY REGION

L. Knobloch

PHILIP CODD
Group Public Relations Officer
BUPA

Dealing with queries from the public is an essential part of BUPA's business. Some queries, however, are less simple than others.

---

4 May 1971

Dear Sirs,

I recently had a full medical check-up at your BUPA Medical Centre and they asked on a pamphlet had I any suggestions.

1. I think the gruesome short dressing-gowns the men have to wear are very very embarrassing and I think full length dressing-gowns, down to the ankle, ought to be supplied.

2. Did the test I had include a test for cancer?

3. What types of cancer do they look for? Also I do not think I had a heart x-ray.

I wonder if you could answer me these questions.

Yours faithfully,
SPIKE MILLIGAN

Dear Mr Milligan,   6 May 1971

Thank you for your letter and the helpful suggestions that you have made.

We find the problem of dressing-gowns an ever recurring source of difficulty. People either complain that they are too short or too long and it seems impossible to be able to suit everybody.

As you know, there is no specific test which can exclude cancer. However, the blood tests that you have sometimes give an indication of this and yours were, of course, quite normal. The x-ray of your chest is a very good screening for cancer of the lung and sometimes the straight x-ray of the abdomen can give an indication of abnormality.

You had an x-ray of your heart and also an electrocardiograph which gives evidence of heart disease and these were both normal in your case.

I hope this satisfactorily answers your questions and once again may I thank you for having taken the trouble to write to us. It is constructive criticism such as yours which enables us to improve our service.

Yours sincerely,
Sidney Kay MD
Medical Director

7 May 1971

Dear Dr Kay,

Thank you for your letter of 6th May.

I think I can sort out your problem of the dressing-gowns. Why not have one long and one short gown in each cubicle?

Sincerely,
SPIKE MILLIGAN

10 May 1971

Dear Mr Milligan,

Thank you very much for your excellent suggestion. It may create some difficulties with people who are what are described as of average size. However, I will certainly tell our receptionist to ask people if they would particularly like a long or a short dressing-gown and try to suit them accordingly.

I made myself very ill laughing at the repeat of your programme on television the other night and am not a little disappointed that when you were here we did not diagnose that you are suffering from 'earthquakes' in the very early stages of this very serious condition!

Yours sincerely,
Sidney Kay MD
Medical Director

Dear Dr Kay,   17 May 1971

Do you know that most average sizes of people are tall or short? I think that the size you should have is average, tall or short, dressing-gowns which would fit everybody.

I have just been to Naples to see Vesuvius and would you believe it the bloody fools have let it go out.

Sincerely,
SPIKE MILLIGAN

53

19 May 1971

Dear Mr Milligan,

Thank you once again for your helpful note.

We have given the matter further consideration and decided that probably our best course is to tackle patients' knees. It seems to us that some form of knee disguise may well prove to be a most effective answer and avoid all embarrassment. If they were not recognizable as knees then people would not really worry as to what they are seeing.

How unfortunate for you to have been to Naples and to have found Vesuvius out!

Yours sincerely,
Sidney Kay, MD
Medical Director

Dear Dr Kay,

21 May 1971

The Case of the Difficult Dressing-Gowns

The knees' disguise is all very well but supposing somebody walks around the back, what then? Oh no, sir, if the knee is to be disguised and the back of the knee left in existence a false plastic knee will have to be fitted to the back of the leg to prevent an optical illusion when the man has his legs in the reverse position to his body. But then, the moment he kneels down for his cholesterol count the whole game is given away and the knee disguise revealed for what it is, a flagrant forgery. No, I propose that we have floor length dressing-gowns and then a 2 ft dwarf will be inserted in the wearer's insteps to give the impression of mobility.

I hope this is all clear to you – I have opened a file called 'The BUPA Affair'.

Good news. As you know, they have transferred the fire from Vesuvius to Mt Etna which is working beautifully. Book now for the third San Francisco, due any minute.

Sincerely,
SPIKE MILLIGAN

KEITH QUINN
Marketing Manager – Petfoods
The Nestlé Company Limited

The makers of Anadin might ponder on a lesson from a poster they developed for an Arab market. Their poster featured, left to right, a picture of a woman in obvious pain, moving to a centre shot of her reaching for her Anadin and resolving itself into a final shot of her in blissful relief. A good direct treatment for Anadin, you might think, except that Arabs read right to left! No doubt brand share among Arab masochists reached record heights.

JOHN NELLIGAN
Managing Director
Britannia Music Company Limited

Chasing an overdue account, I received the following note:

'I refer to the enclosed account in respect of goods supplied to my wife. I have told you before that my wife has left me, she has left her family, and no longer lives at the address printed on your statement. If you should catch up with her before I do, would you ask her what she has done with my track suit and rugger boots.'

GRAHAM WALSH
Director
Premier Brands UK Limited

Two or three years ago our factory at Knighton, in Staffordshire, was visited by the local environmental officer after a complaint from a nearby farmer. The complaint concerned the open burning of some of our packaging waste. The environmental officer ordered us to stop the burning immediately.

We were obliged to hire a contractor to remove our rubbish in special skips which also had to be provided by us.

Some weeks later he was casually asked what he had done with the rubbish.

He said he had taken it to a local farmer (yes, the same one) who then burnt it for a fee!

Naturally, we informed the environmental officer who soon put a stop to his lucrative bonfires.

Chapter 4

The Travel Business

LORD KING OF WARTNABY
Chairman of British Airways

An old Vickers Viking was flying from Khartoum to London. The range of the aircraft was short and it made a number of stops along the Mediterranean coast before flying across France to London. The heating inside the cabin was maintained by a small control – very much like an ordinary radiator control – operated by a stewardess. Before each of the stops in Africa, where the ground temperature was well in the nineties, the stewardess turned off the heating inside the cabin. But on arrival in London the weather was very cold so she left the heating on. As the aircraft began its descent to Heathrow a little old lady in the front row of the cabin turned reproachfully to the stewardess and said, 'Now, dear, don't forget to lower the undercarriage.'

A J CUMMING
Director – Advertising
Austin Rover Group Limited

Austin Rover was running a Mini advertising campaign in 1980, with posters and advertisements that had headlines such as:

> *Nips in and out like Ronald Biggs.*
> *Does a better turn than Fiona Richmond.*

At a time when oil prices were volatile, and Sheikh Yamani of Saudi Arabia was never out of the headlines, the agency proposed to highlight the Mini's economy with the slogan:

> *At 48.5 mpg, it will give you a run for Yamani.*

Nobody thought we would get permission to run the line but fortunately an enterprising lady in Leo Burnett had the cheek to send a telex to Sheikh Yamani asking his permission.

To our surprise and delight, we received the following reply from Mr Ibrahim Khaberi in Sheikh Yamani's office giving us permission to run the line.

The advertising ran and contributed to one of the best known advertising campaigns in the Mini's long life.

29.1.80

ATTENTION SHEIKH YAMANI

I WOULD BE GRATEFUL IF YOU COULD CONTACT ME TO DISCUSS THE POSSIBILITY OF USING YOUR NAME IN A PRESS AND POSTER CAMPAIGN TO ADVERTISE THE AUSTIN MORRIS MINI CAR. THE PROPOSED CAMPAIGN IS A PICTURE OF AN AUSTIN MORRIS MINI WITH THE LINE 'AT 48.5 MPG IT'LL GIVE YOU A RUN FOR YAMANI'. MY TELEPHONE NUMBER IN LONDON IS 836 2424. / I LOOK FORWARD TO YOUR REPLY. / THANKING YOU IN ANTICIPATION. / REGARDS.

VALERIE HODSON – CASTING OFFICE

11 FEB 1980

ATTN: VALERIE HODSON
CASTING OFFICE

RYT DATED 29 JANUARY 1980 ADDRESSED TO HIS EXCELLENCY SHEIKH AHMED ZAKI YAMANI SUGGESTING TO USE HIS NAME IN A PRESS AND POSTER CAMPAIGN TO ADVERTISE AUSTIN MORRIS MINI CAR (STOP) I AM PLEASED TO INFORM YOU THAT HIS EXCELLENCY HAS NO OBJECTION TO YOUR SUGGESTION.

BEST WISHES

IBRAHIM KHABERI
DIRECTOR GENERAL
MINISTER'S OFFICE

PETER HARRAND
Assistant General Manager, Marketing
National and Provincial

The National and Provincial has a branch in the heart of tourist London, and on one busy day a rather loud Texan asked a member of staff to step outside, where he pointed to St Paul's Cathedral and said: 'Is that St Paul's Cathedral?' The assistant said it was. 'Tell me dear, is it open on Sunday?'

JOHN PETERSEN
Vice President
American Express Europe

When I used to work at Trust House Forte, I ws shocked to discover that among the different categories of catering operation was one described as 'Terminal Catering'. This was the term for the catering provided at airports.

SIDNEY WEIGHELL
Former General Secretary
National Union of Railwaymen

Early in 1978 I was invited to visit China.

At that time very few visitors were allowed into China because of the problems created by Chairman Mao Tse Tung's cultural revolution. I accepted the invitation eagerly.

The programme for my twenty-six day visit had been designed to enable me to travel extensively throughout China. I was obviously interested in their railways and was given every facility to travel over the network, which is, excluding bicycles, the principal form of travel for the Chinese people.

I was first shown round Peking Railway Station, which looks not unlike Euston and where hundreds of train travellers stood in long queues at numerous ticket windows.

One of the queues was very much shorter than the others and I asked why. My Chinese interpreter explained that the longer queues were for the hard seats, the short queue was for the soft seats.

I was quite puzzled by this reply, but decided to wait till I got on the train to find out the answer.

Eventually we were taken to the train and took our seats in a very elegant carriage with seating arrangements similar to trains in Britain. My interpreter explained that this was a soft seat carriage. I asked to be shown a hard seat carriage and further along the train I found hard wooden seats together with hard wooden tables.

I then asked about the cost of travel between the soft seats and the hard seats and was told there was a significant difference in the price. To which I replied: 'That is first class and second class travel.' 'No,' insisted my interpreter, 'there are no classes in China, just soft seats and hard seats.'

THE BISHOP OF
ST ALBANS

When I was a curate at Morden in Surrey, there was a great demand for weddings at the old parish church of St Lawrence. So much so that weddings were timed at forty-five minute intervals on most Saturdays. We used to impress upon the brides and bridegrooms that they must not on any account arrive late at the church or they would be told to wait and put to the end of the queue. One particular Saturday when I was on wedding duty the 3 o'clock bride did not turn up until 3.23 p.m.

She had a perfectly good explanation. The wedding car had broken down in Tooting and she was the tearful victim of circumstances. Another bride was due at 3.45 p.m. and in this instance I could not make her wait until the end of the queue because there were weddings at 4.30 p.m. and 5.15 p.m. and it is against the law to solemnise a marriage after 6 p.m.

I therefore offered the bride and bridegroom the shortest and quickest service I could devise, if they were ready for it. They agreed, and off we went at a cracking pace.

We had only one hymn instead of two, I missed out a bit here and a bit there and to their relief I was able to get them out of the church to the strains of the Wedding March at exactly 3.44 p.m. As their congregation went out of the church, the 3.45 p.m. congregation came in by another door and the next wedding started bang on time.

It was a triumph of organization ... but I still have a few lingering worries about whether they were legally married!

MOSS EVANS
Former General Secretary
Transport and General Workers' Union

In the fifties, my union was not prepared to provide motor cars for district officials.

Other unions in the engineering or motor industries were more generous – or extravagant depending on your point of view – to their officials, who often used to give us lifts to and from joint meetings.

I was in my Birmingham office one day preparing to leave for a meeting at Rover in Solihull. As I got up to leave, a rather unhappy member with a problem walked into my office. I asked him if he would walk with me to the bus stop so I could listen to his tale of woe. He agreed and gathered up his bicycle which was leaning against a wall outside the office.

As we were walking down Broad Street, the driver of a large black Vauxhall tooted his horn.

'I am most impressed!' he said. 'Your union is really going places!'

I asked him what he meant, and he said: 'Well, not only do they now provide you with a handsome bicycle, they even supply a man to push it for you.'

MARTIN HUDSON
Director
PGL Young Adventure Holidays Limited

Youngsters joining our adventure holidays from abroad sometimes stay with an escort agency, until we can transport them to the adventure centres.

On one such occasion a young Israeli boy was taken to the home of the lady running the agency and invited to have a look around the garden, which had an ornamental pond. When his hostess was not watching, he slid his hand into the water, plucked out a fish, and ate it! We know this is true because we got a bill for £1.80 for the goldfish consumed!

THE REVD
THE LORD SOPER
West London Mission of the Methodist Church

The trouble with preaching in the open air is that people love to interrupt. One Sunday afternoon in Hyde Park at Speakers' Corner, I was answering a question about the Kingdom of Heaven, as some evangelists across the Atlantic proclaimed it, when I was interrupted by someone in the crowd who claimed that I was misrepresenting the facts. I asked him whether he had been to the USA, as I had quite recently. He said he had not, whereupon I advised him not to talk about matters of which he was uninformed. His response was unexpected and devastating. He wanted to know whether I had been to heaven. I had to say no, to which he replied, 'Then don't *you* talk of things you know nothing about.'

IAN BROOKE
International Co-ordinator, Lights
Bryant & May

Between 1914 and 1917 Swan Vestas introduced a unique accident life insurance policy, inserted into every box of Swan Vestas matches. The main condition of the insurance was that a box of Swan Vestas had to be found on the injured person at the time of the accident, and that death had to be due to injuries sustained whilst travelling.

'Quite frankly, Digby, we'd prefer you not to wear our name on your vest during this year's Marathon... we've had a look at your medical report...'

Chapter 5

The Advertising Business

GEOFFREY ELTON
Novaction (UK) Limited

Brian was sent out to one of the banana states in Central America to advise on a particular problem that had been encountered in researching a certain market.

There were several key issues that had to be addressed:

— How to persuade respondents to attend a hall test (it was a police state and any invitation was likely to be received with deep suspicion – if not terror).

— How to ensure that, if people could be persuaded to attend, that they would actually honour the commitment so to do, as they were notoriously unreliable.

As Brian had been received as nothing short of *the* market research guru, he felt that particularly creative measures were required.

His first bright idea was to contact a local priest and ask if the church could be used as a hall testing facility. The priest agreed, for a handsome donation, and thus the matter of suspicion was overcome.

To conquer the problem of ensuring that those who said they were prepared to attend did so, Brian arranged for a television personality to be in attendance and to personally welcome each respondent.

Having got respondents to church, the next problem that emerged was a cultural issue of respondents not wishing to disagree or say anything bad about the ideas being tested. Brian's final piece of inventiveness was to instruct the interviewers to point at the crucifix in the church immediately after asking any of the potentially problem questions, thereby encouraging each respondent to be quite truthful in answering them.

ALLEN SHEPPARD
Chairman
Grand Metropolitan

Two or three years ago we were running a series of advertisements for Smirnoff Vodka. One of the lines we liked most was: 'I used to think the Kama Sutra was an Indian restaurant until I discovered Smirnoff'. We always undertake research before launching a new advertising campaign and did not run the advertisement as nearly everyone asked thought that the Kama Sutra *was* an Indian restaurant!

ANNE MENZIES
Head of Product Development
English Tourist Board

Apparently the Women's Farmers Union produced a number of posters to encourage us all to buy British produce. A poster featuring a hand holding up a large shopping basket found its way into the gents' loo at a London station. Strategically placed above the urinals it said: 'The future of Britain . . . is in your hands'!

SIR EDWARD GUINNESS
Guinness PLC

It is said that when S H Benson Ltd were chosen as our Advertising Agency in 1972, Mr Oswald Greene, the Chairman of that company, said that this would, of course, be one of their most important accounts, and asked for a little time in which to prepare his campaign.

Some months later, Mr Greene with his team sat opposite the Chairman, Mr Case and his directors in the boardroom at St James's Gate. 'And what have you got for us Mr Greene?' said Mr Case. Mr Greene fumbled in his waistcoat pocket and produced a little piece of paper folded up many times. He slowly unfolded it and then read out the words, 'Guinness is good for you.' 'And is that all you have got for us after three months' work?' asked Mr Case.

JON STOWELL
Marketing Director
Van den Berghs and Jurgens Ltd

In the sixties there was a Persil commercial which opened with a shot from outside a window as a small girl wiped away the frost from the inside. As she did so, she drew her mother's attention to the snow and frost outside with the line 'Mummy, look! Everything's gone white outside.'

On the day of the shoot all went well. The child was adorable and a great little actress. The only problem was her voice. It in no way fitted her angelic looks and cosy middle class environment. The director put the film in the can anyway and told his producer to line up a succession of young girls for the sound studios where the line could be dubbed in over the original voice.

The dubbing session began badly. The director and the sound man found it more difficult than they expected to explain to each young tot the intricacies of sound dubbing in synchronization with the lip movements projected on the screen. Child after child failed to execute the delicate task, and the film maker became more and more desperate. Eventually, after hours of catastrophe, one very small child remained to be tried. The director began the most careful and elaborate explanation of what the task involved. He had just reached the point where he was explaining that 'when you see the crayon line move across the picture, you say ...', when she interrupted his flow by remarking wearily, 'Oh, I see, you want me to post synch it.'

Five minutes later, the job was done.

ANONYMOUS

Charles Saatchi is a man of legendary shyness. When the agency were pitching for Singer, a very important prospective, Charles dodged the meeting, but was so desperate to know how the pitch was progressing that he kept peering through the projection windows into the crowded presentation theatre. By early evening, with the meeting still in full swing, he gave up and went home, only to return an hour or so later in casual clothes to discuss the outcome with his staff. As he entered the reception area, the door from the theatre swung open and the prospective client emerged with a throng of agency people. Desperate to avoid an introduction, Charles picked up a duster lying on the reception desk and flicked it around.

Maurice noticed and called out:

'You can do my office when you've finished here.'

JOHN CUTLER
Product Manager
Wander Limited

The nostalgic 'Ovaltineys' commercials, set around the time of the abdication, aroused great interest when they were first screened in 1975. Members of the public phoned in claiming they were the artistes who had appeared in these commercials in their youth. One woman tried to charge us repeat fees, and threatened to sue us if we didn't pay her. Little did she know that the film had been made earlier that year.

NORMAN C BERRY
President
Ogilvy & Mather Advertising, New York

Overheard on another set while making a film for cinema, circa 1955:

First woman: Mine's all hard and scratchy
Second woman: Mine's all soft and silky
First woman: What do you do with yours?
Second woman: Oh, just dip and squeeze, dip and squeeze

The product being advertised was Lux Flakes. The thing being 'dipped and squeezed' was a woman's pullover.

BOB RIVERS
Consultant

Some years ago in the West Country, I accompanied a salesman on the first day of the launch of Wilkinson Sword After Shave. Our objective was to sell a half-dozen to each retail chemist.

At our first call the conversation went:

Salesman: 'Good afternoon, Mr Bloggs, I have specially called on you today to introduce you to Wilkinson Sword's latest product, Wilkinson Sword After Shave.'

Mr Bloggs: 'I don't want any.'

Salesman: 'But Mr Bloggs, this is going to become the brand leader in the After Shave market, and will receive massive TV support.'

Mr Bloggs: 'I've already told you, I don't want any!'

Salesman: 'All I want you to take is a half-dozen from the car to satisfy the undoubted consumer demand that my company will create.'

Mr Bloggs: 'Look son, this is the last time, I've told you once, I've told you twice and I'm telling you now, if you were to stand here until Christmas, you would still get no order.'

Salesman: 'What are we having, turkey or duck?'

ROSS SOUTHWELL
Sales and Marketing Director
Newforge Foods

The actor and the dog were extremely tired, and the dog was rather full.

It was the final scene to be shot for a pet food advertisement.

After twenty unsuccessful takes, with the actor muffing his one line time after time, he got it right.

Everyone breathed heavy sighs of relief until the sound man took his earphones off: 'Sorry Harv, we'll have to do it again.'

KATHY CUDDIHY
Public Relations Manager
Cow & Gate

We launched a non-pasteurized double cream, from
Devon, into a post war market dominated by tinned
single sterilized cream. Although we decided to launch as
Cow & Gate, the senior marketing man felt Farmer's Wife
was the name people knew from before the war. After
prolonged argument, we compromised with, Cow & Gate,
Farmer's Wife Double Devon Cream. But we failed to
mention the non-pasteurized bit – the key sales advantage.
Hence the tag line, 'it's fresh up from Devon'. Advertising
agencies in those days insisted on including all this in each
TV advert. So we had exchanges like: 'Would you pass the
Cow & Gate, Farmer's Wife Double Devon Cream? It's
fresh up from Devon you know!' 'Ah, I'm afraid we all
made a rush for the Cow & Gate, Farmer's Wife Double
Devon Cream at lunchtime and it's all gone – it tastes so
good being fresh up from Devon.'

At Christmas the TV production company's frustration
boiled over and they produced a send-up version featuring
'Cousin Connie's Charming Country Cottage Choice
Clotted Cream – it comes quickly from Cornwall'.

LEN HEATH
Chairman
Imagination

It's not easy using children in commercials. We had a small boy and a small girl in a fish finger advertisement. They did their best, but it took several takes to get it right. Unfortunately by the time we reached Take 11, the poor boy had eaten at least ten fish fingers. This time we got everything right, the two kids were brilliant, and the crucial moment arrived – whereupon the boy was violently sick!

MIKE HOPKINS
Director of Corporate Affairs
Nabisco Group

I was very impressed when I visited the advertising agency, Hobson Bates and Partners, by a room full of artists' mock-ups for Double Diamond.

Next day, I understand, the Account Director asked his secretary to collect this fortune in design costs from the room. There was no sign of the tins.

Lengthy investigation revealed that the cleaning lady had cleared 'all the empties' the night before and they were on their way to the crusher.

SIR BERNARD AUDLEY
Chairman
AGB Research

Blenkinsop wasn't the brightest of the advertising sales team but you had to give him marks for trying. It's possible he still can't figure out how he blew it. How he actually got in to see the client's Managing Director in the first place was a mystery to us, and a credit to him. Our magazine simply wasn't a natural for domestic appliance advertising.

But Blenkinsop, on a high and playing it straight from the salesman's manual, achieved the impossible. 'I'll tell the agency twelve colour pages,' said the Managing Director.

Blenkinsop remembered page 35 of the manual 'Part on a positive note.' Taking the recommended time to get into his overcoat gave him the opportunity for the clincher. 'Congratulations on your decision, Sir. Now our readers will know what everybody else knows, that Goblin is the best Hoover on the market.'

ANONYMOUS

A new painting, *The Dancers*, had been hung in reception, reputedly the latest addition to Charles Saatchi's famous collection of contemporary art. No one liked it. The final straw was a letter addressed to Charles, supposedly from

the kids of the local adventure playground – a converted
bomb-site behind the agency. It read:

Dear Sir
Please can we have our painting back. We haven't
finished it yet.

PETER HAMBLIN
Director of Marketing
Panasonic UK Limited

We were filming a TV commercial for a Panasonic Music Centre.

The central characters of the commercial were impersonations of the pioneers of audio equipment, Marconi and Edison, who were extolling the virtues of our latest and greatest audio system. As usual it had taken all day and we were still getting nowhere. At last things seemed to be going well, when suddenly a bell rang and totally destroyed the take. 'Edison' raised an eyebrow and murmured: 'It sounds as though Alexander's just invented the telephone.'

BOB HODGES
Director and General Manager
Lyons Tetley

At a food exhibition in the 1970s we were mildly surprised to find a delegation from Bulgaria taking a keen interest in our tea-bags.

We gave them some samples to take home with them, and some weeks later received a letter of thanks from Bulgaria. The tea, they said, was excellent – even if it was rather time consuming opening each bag.

D T HESLOP
HQ Director of Sales
British Gas

A film was being made which involved blowing up a listed manor house. Such was the expense and risk involved it could only be shot once. The director wisely took the precaution of setting up three cameras to shoot the scene on the basis that one out of three should take.

Action. Boom! The house went up. When the results from each camera crew were passed in by walkie talkie radio, they were as follows:

Camera 1: 'Damn. The mechanism has jammed – sorry!'
Camera 2: 'You won't believe this – we're out of film!'
Camera 3: 'Ready when you are squire!'

Chapter 6

The Money Business

RON MILLER
Sales Director
London Weekend Television

Many years ago, at about the time Southern Television went on air, I accompanied a very aggressive sales executive to Goddards Polishes, who in desperation promised to spend £400 if the agency, Colman Prentice & Varley, were agreeable.

I fixed up a meeting with the agency and took the eager young salesman with me. The agency gave all sorts of reasons why £400 would do nothing for the product in the southern region but my man would have none of it. Eventually in desperation an account director said:

'If we spend £400 on Southern Television, we would probably sell two tins of Goddards Polish.' To which my colleague replied:

'So you would agree with me that the campaign would not be a total waste of money!'

STUART RANSOM
Chief Manager
Lloyds Bank

One of our farming customers paid in £25,000 – in cash. To the cashier's surprise the cash was contained in a milk churn.

When the cashier had finished counting the money, she said: 'I'm sorry, but there is £26,000 here.'

'Oh,' said the farmer, 'I must have brought in the wrong churn.'

WILLIAM O'CONNELL
Branch Manager
Barclays Bank PLC

At the time of the sovereign lending crisis, a branch had written to a private customer to tell him he was overdrawn. The customer wrote:

'I take great exception to your letter advising the overdraft situation, as it occurred as a complete accident. I further take exception to the tone of your letter which seemed to me to lack originality and was purely stereotype. Presumably you do not write to your larger customers such as Brazil and Mexico, who borrow substantial amounts, in such a manner.'

The rather banal reply was that the branch had written but surprisingly the letters had been returned 'gone away'.

'Another letter from Barclays Bank, Brighton about our
National Overdraft, Presidente. Shall I return it marked
'gone away' or send a team of hit men?'

HARRY SOLOMAN
Chairman
Hillsdown Holdings PLC

A kind shareholder telephoned to let us know that a letter from us containing some bulky documents did not have sufficient postage and he had had to pay 30p excess. He was very polite and said he had telephoned because he thought other shareholders might have had the same problem. In fact they did. I thanked him and then wrote letters enclosing stamps to the value of 30p.

I was surprised to hear from him again to tell me that he had received my letter with the stamps inside, but unfortunately the envelope had not been stamped!

'It's agreed then that we'll draw straws to see who breaks the news at the Annual Meeting.'

JOHN HANDFORTH
Assistant General Manager
Leeds Building Society

When building societies decided to cast off their fuddy-duddy image and go in for dynamic marketing, the Leeds was not going to be left behind.

A new advertising campaign was developed using the potential ambiguity in the word 'Bond', with specific reference being made to Ian Fleming's fictional hero. The ad, supposedly filmed inside the Kremlin, featured the archetypal KGB hireling apparently complaining to his chief ... something about 'Bond'. The ad was filmed in Russian dialogue with 'Bond' being one of the very few decipherable English words.

The chief says, *'James* Bond?' to which the hireling replies, 'No, Leeds Permanent *High Return* Bond!' Then the full details of that account appeared on the screen, with the figures 007 (James Bond's 'License to Kill' prefix code) being replaced by the account's interest rate.

We all thought it was brilliant and the ad was placed on the TV schedules.

Its maiden appearance was in the prestigious centre-break of 'News at Ten' ... minutes after that programme's extended and detailed coverage of the Russians' shooting down of the Korean airliner number 007.

LWT were bombarded with calls from irate viewers appalled by the company's insensitivity.

The head of LWT had to make an unscheduled appearance on one of his own programmes to explain the situation and defend the showing of the commercial.

We put further showings on hold. But there were those who still believed that the Leeds had deliberately prepared an ad which capitalized on the disaster.

SIR JOHN BOYD, CBE

Former General Secretary
Amalgamated Union of Engineering Workers

I had a date at 11 Downing Street with Jim Callaghan when he was Chancellor of the Exchequer. As I had to go on from there to important wage negotiations and time was pressing, the Chancellor graciously offered me the use of an official Government car. Unfortunately I knew there would be a fair-sized demonstration of my union members at the employers' offices, and with wage-restraint the issue of the moment, it wouldn't do for me to arrive in a Government car. So I had to decline.

In friendly spirit, Jim Callaghan decided to walk me to the end of Downing Street, where, hailing a taxi, he instructed the driver to take me to the Embankment.

You can imagine my embarrassment when I discovered I had failed to transfer my wallet from one suit to another, and had only one shilling in my pocket.

As we sped along I told the driver of my predicament. 'Blimey mate!' he said. 'You've just left the bloody Chancellor and you try to tell me you've got no money. Well, get out quick.' With that, he bundled me out on to the street to walk the remaining three-quarters of a mile.

'All of our best brains are going to America. We offered
them a company car.'

'Take a prayer, Miss Hobday...'

Chapter 7

The Drinks Business

DEBBIE STYLES
Public Relations Executive
Watney Combe Reid & Truman

In 1986 a group of sailors from HMS *Jupiter*, temporarily stationed in London, enjoyed a prolonged visit to Watney Combe Reid's Mortlake brewery. No ale or lager was left unsampled. The following day HMS *Jupiter* became famous by colliding with Tower Bridge. Who says Watney's beer is weak?

JOHN GORMAN
Marketing Manager
CPC (UK) Ltd

We wanted new product ideas for Frank Cooper. After flavoured marmalades we came to bottled water. Mineral water was a young and dynamic sector, and seemed an ideal product if we could find a suitable source.

Many brands were appearing bearing the name of the spring they were bottled from; we just had to find one for us.

The name of a splendidly prestigious spa in the West of England came suddenly to mind. The consensus, however, was that Frank Cooper's Bath Water wouldn't quite do!

KEITH QUINN
Marketing Manager – Petfoods
The Nestlé Company Limited

They weren't sure what to make of Pepsi-Cola in Japan. When the famous 'come alive with Pepsi' slogan was first translated into Japanese, it appeared to offer more than your average beverage. Apparently, to the Japanese, the slogan meant 'raise your ancestors from the dead with Pepsi'.

DENIS URQUHART
Chairman, Marketing
Bass PLC

My favourite television commercial was 25 years ago, for a brand of stout that no longer exists, long before sexism had been invented. It went like this:

Two yokels in a bar. Yokel smocks etc – Northern accents.

First Yokel: 'Why is a Milkmaid Stout like a stout milkmaid?'
Second Yokel: 'I dunno. Why is a Milkmaid Stout like a stout milkmaid?'
First Yokel: 'Cos 'er's got a fluffy head – and a good body – and yer can stay with 'er till the cows come home.'

What happy days – before Codes of Practice!

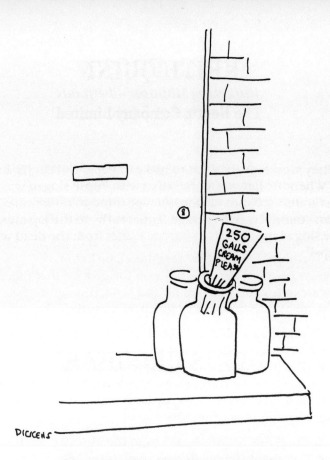

DICKENS

MAC MacPHERSON
Brand Development Manager
International Distillers and Vintners

It was the first time Baileys had been produced on a large scale. Blenders blended, whiskey waited, stainless steel gleamed. We were anxiously waiting for the missing component which was around 250 gallons of fresh double cream. Probably the largest single delivery the up-country dairy had ever made until then. Enough of it to bathe in. My stomping around was interrupted by a quiet, diffident voice: 'Excuse me, sorr, the milkman's here.'

ROBIN FROST
Head of Public Relations
Harveys of Bristol

In 1949 the Ministry of Food drew Harveys' attention to Regulation One of the Defence (Sales of Food) Regulations 1943, which made it an offence to mislead the public about the nature or nutritional value of any food.

'In the Ministry's opinion,' the letter said, 'the use of the wording "Bristol Milk" might well be held to contravene the said regulations on the ground that this indicates the presence of milk and as such suggests that the wine has certain special nutritive qualities.'

The company responded by pointing out that the name Bristol Milk had been in existence 300 years longer than the Ministry of Food, and suggested the Ministry's objection must logically apply to Bristol Cream and hence 'to all shaving creams, face creams, boot creams etc, as suggesting they have nutritive value'.

Nothing further was heard from the Ministry on this subject. Perhaps the officials were placated less by the elegance of the company's argument than by its figures: four years after the end of the war, exports of Harveys Bristol Cream and Bristol Milk were worth 500,000 dollars a year from America and Canada alone.

E A TASKER
Director of External Affairs
Saccone & Speed Limited

I was lecturing to trade students on the subject of port wines.

Having explained that the grapes were grown in the upper Douro and that the wine was made there in the various farms or quintas, I then went on to tell them that the new port was brought down in the pipes in the following spring for maturation in the lodges in Via Nova de Gaia.

At question time one of the students asked how long were these pipes!

MAC MacPHERSON
Brand Development Manager
International Distillers and Vintners

We were assembling the first production plant for Baileys Irish Cream, and we were on a tight budget.

I rang the production engineer to get a vital spare part.

'Tell me the plate numbers,' he said.

Five minutes of technical details.

'Yes we can make those up for you.'

'Any chance of getting them before next Thursday?'

Three second silence.

'I'm afraid we couldn't do anything like that for six months at least.'

Five second silence.

'I wonder if you use any of our products, a couple of bottles of Red Breast Whiskey maybe?'

Three second silence.

'We couldn't do it all this afternoon, sir, could you ever come over in the morning?'

STEPHEN WELLS
Managing Director
Connexions Market Research

In an effort to arrest a decline in sherry sales, a shipper was researching the appeal of new sherry-based products. For one woman, no such new products were required, as she claimed that she and all her friends had given up both sweet and dry products and plumped for new 'Armadillo' sherry.

Chapter 8

The
Food
Business

BOB HODGES
Director and General Manager
Lyons Tetley

A head buyer went to see the sales director of a food manufacturing company, based at an impressive country house.

A large Alsatian greeted him. When he went to open the door, the dog followed him all the way to the sales director's office.

The sales director showed no surprise, and the dog sat down on the floor. A few minutes later the dog moved into the corner of the plush office where he deposited a large pile. Both the sales director and the head buyer tried to ignore it.

At the end of the meeting, in an increasingly pungent atmosphere, the head buyer got up to leave and the Alsatian trotted out with him. 'Do you want the dog in or out?' asked the buyer. 'Oh,' said the sales director. 'I thought he was yours!'

A M MARSH
Marketing Director
Rowntree Mackintosh

A crisis meeting was taking place in the Managing Director's office at which the possibility was being discussed that a major brand might have to be withdrawn temporarily from sale. Discussion had gone on for two hours; the directors were in despair with their heads in their hands when the secretary came in bearing tea. After passing round the cups she went out and whispered, 'Don't worry gentlemen, they're only sweeties!'

PETER MOSELEY

Marketing Director
HP Foods

When Harold Wilson and his wife Mary were interviewed shortly after he had become Prime Minister in 1964, Mary Wilson complained about his habit of covering everything she cooked with HP sauce.

The Prime Minister puffed at his pipe, neither confirming nor denying the story. HP was generally considered a working-class taste. If, therefore, the belief that he was devoted to the sauce established his credentials as a man of the people, so be it. As for HP Sauce itself, not only was it receiving publicity on a scale undreamed of by its advertising agents, but its links with Parliament were now incontrovertible.

In 1975, HP was a hundred years old.

To mark the occasion a great banquet was arranged. Two hundred guests were headed by Harold Wilson. The savoury was 'La Croute aux Oeufs Sauce HP'. The time came for speeches.

After congratulating the company and urging it to further efforts in the export market, Mr Wilson paused, before making a confession. Contrary to popular belief, it was not HP but Lea & Perrins Worcestershire Sauce to which he was particularly partial. Poor HP Sauce! At such a moment, to be outshone by its social superior!

Garland

FRANK SAXBY
Director
Saxby Brothers

The Saxby's stand at the Ideal Home Exhibition was most impressive – notably the several large dummy pies ranged in the background, with 1 lb and smaller pies on offer on the counter.

One admiring customer asked for a 'large pie' for a special party. The assistant duly wrapped and sold a large pie.

We got a phone call some time later from a tearful and furious customer. She had cut the pie in front of her guests and out flowed ... sawdust! She wasn't easily pacified.

JOHN PETERSEN
Vice President
American Express Europe

When I was working as a relief van salesman selling bread and cakes in the Welsh Valleys, I once delivered a tray of bread and cakes to a very small country shop, shut the back door of the van and drove back to the Cardiff depot. On arrival I opened the van door to check the stock, and out jumped an extremely fat sheep. There was no other stock left.

DOMINIC CADBURY
Chief Executive
Cadbury Schweppes

Cadbury's used to run an advertising poster depicting cows grazing happily in a meadow.

The accompanying copyline assured consumers that 10,000 of these cows were working at Bournville to produce Cadbury's Dairy Milk.

The women working on the Bournville production line were not entirely happy about this.

ELIZABETH JONES
Archivist
Colman's of Norwich

Jeremiah Colman, who founded the firm in the early nineteenth century, was a shrewd man. One Sunday morning he was keeping an eye on a young man he thought was after the ducks' eggs. When the lad came up, he said, 'What! Have you been after my eggs?' 'No, Sir.' 'Oh,' said Mr Colman, 'then you are an honester man than I thought.' In saying this, he hit him on the hat, which was full of eggs, and the stuff ran all down the boy's face.

ADRIAN BOURNE
General Marketing Manager
The Nestlé Company Limited

As a raw consumer (and naïve assistant brand manager), I wrote complaining to J Sainsbury about a fly discovered embedded in their frozen broccoli. Two weeks later I joined Ross Foods to find, as one of my first tasks, a response to one of our major Private Label customers regarding a complaint from Mr Bourne who had found a foreign body in his broccoli.

BEV STOKES
Chairman
George Bassett Foods

I received the following letter from a twelve-year-old boy:

Dear Mr Bassett,

The other day, my Gran gave me my birthday present, which, when I unwrapped it, I saw was one of your 1 lb boxes of Liquorice Allsorts.

The box was already open and there were no coconut ones in it. Is this a mistake in your factory or is my Gran a thief?

We assured him it must have been a mistake at the factory, and sent him a box of coconut ones. Gran's reputation, we hope, remained unsullied.

ALISTAIR WHALLEY
Marketing Manager
The Wrigley Company Limited

In 1975 Wrigley's ran a promotion offering inflatable dummy packs of Wrigley's Spearmint gum 'just like the ones people were carrying under their arms on television'. The response was very good and the orders flooded in ... including one from an old age pensioner who asked, 'Please can you send mine blown-up as I haven't much breath at my age!'

Chapter 9

The
Power
Business

LORD WILSON OF RIEVAULX

House of Lords

With some reluctance, I must credit the Tories for one of my favourite jokes.

I was at the TUC Conference, getting out of the car in front of a crowd of photographers, when my pocket caught fire – from the pipe I had just been smoking.

The Tories used the photograph mercilessly in the following election campaign. The caption read: 'He has burned a hole in his pocket; don't let him burn one in yours.'

DAVID STEEL MP

House of Commons

During the days of the Lib-Lab pact, I had many meetings with the Prime Minister, Jim Callaghan. On one occasion I drove with my two assistants to Number 10 feeling very statesmanlike.

Such feelings were quickly dispelled when we came to leave and the car would not start. I know that politicians like to cling to power, but I must be the only one to have to be physically pushed out of Downing Street.

CECIL PARKINSON MP

House of Commons

After I left Cambridge I became a management trainee with Metal Box, a large industrial company employing more than 30,000 people. When I had been with the company a couple of months, I was invited to London to a party. When I met my hosts' next-door-neighbour, he recognized my tie and asked me what my job was. I told him I was working for this large industrial concern which, because it sold very little directly to the public, was not particularly well-known. I asked him if he had ever heard of Metal Box. He had indeed; he happened to be its managing director.

The fact that I left his employ a few months later is entirely coincidental.

'Thank God his work experience finishes on Friday.'

SIR TERENCE BECKETT

formerly CBI

Diplomacy has traditionally relied on a language of codes and hidden meanings. Hence Metternich at the Congress of Vienna, when told of the sudden death of the Russian Ambassador, was reputed to have said, 'What did he mean by that?'

Industrial relations in Britain have their own set of protocols that enable essential messages to be transmitted, while maintaining the requisite appearance of robust hostility.

I remember in one round of negotiations with the unions, we had made a counter-offer which was far below their original claim. They said they were shocked, bitterly disappointed and they utterly rejected our counter-offer as a completely inadequate response. I said to my industrial relations director, a man of long experience in these affairs, that this looked bad, didn't it? 'No,' he said. 'It's very promising. They didn't say they were humiliated, did they?'

LEN MURRAY

House of Lords

When I was TUC General Secretary, Terry Parry, General Secretary of the Brigades Union, came in to tell me that his Executive had decided to take industrial action. I was worried about the effect on public safety, but they said: 'Don't worry, Len, we're adopting the policy of the cross-eyed javelin thrower.' 'What the devil's that?' I asked. 'Well,' said Terry, 'we shan't withdraw all fire cover in any area at any time. We shall pull one or two brigades out for a few hours, then they will go back in and others will come out. So there will always be cover for emergencies.' 'And what's that got to do with throwing javelins?' I asked. 'This way,' replied Terry, 'the cross-eyed javelin thrower may not win many first prizes, but by God he keeps the crowd on its toes!'

DAVID HARRIS
General Manager
The Nestlé Company Limited

When we built a new factory in Ulster, the local fishermen complained that we were taking too much of their river water for use in the plant. We decided therefore to sink an artesian well, and contacted the local water diviner. He duly arrived, complete with hazel switch, and after a few minutes' walking across the spare land beside the factory the switch behaved as if it were alive. 'Dig here and you'll find water,' he declared, and so we began drilling. In no time at all a great spurt of water leapt from the ground. Unfortunately, we had struck the main water pipe supplying the local railway station. The Irish diviner looked on with pride and said, 'I'm never wrong. I told you there was water down there!'

SUSAN BLOW
Management Training Consultant
MAST

The elegant lady had sat quietly during the dinner party while the pompous and self-opinionated old gentleman to her right systematically put the universe to rights from soup to dessert. Finally, he turned to her. 'And tell me, my dear, what do you do all day to amuse yourself?'

To which she replied: 'Silly me's a judge.'

J C C BROWN
Director of Corporate Relations
British Telecom

Spike Milligan wrote to British Telecom Chairman Sir George Jefferson, complaining about the early morning noise of drilling from engineers digging up the road outside his house.

'I've been tempted to set fire to their equipment,' he told Sir George.

Mr Milligan received a prompt reply from the Chairman, apologizing, and promising action to stop the early morning noise.

Enclosed with the letter was a box of matches. 'Just in case my instructions are ignored!'